MASTERING PYTHON

From Basics to Advanced Techniques

Yatendra Kumar Singh 'Manuh'

CONTENTS

INTRODUCTION

Welcome to "Mastering Python: From Basics to Advanced Techniques", your comprehensive guide to becoming proficient in Python programming. Whether you are a novice just starting out or an experienced programmer looking to deepen your knowledge, this book is designed to provide you with the tools and understanding needed to excel in the world of Python.

Python is a versatile and powerful programming language that is widely used in various fields such as web development, data science, artificial intelligence, machine learning, and more. Its simplicity and readability make it an excellent choice for beginners, while its extensive libraries and frameworks make it indispensable for professionals.

In this book, we will journey through the vast landscape of Python, starting with the fundamental concepts and gradually progressing to more advanced topics. Each chapter is crafted to build upon the previous ones, ensuring a smooth and logical progression of learning.

Here's what you can expect:

Chapter 1-5: We begin with the basics, covering essential concepts such as variables, data types, control structures, and functions. These chapters lay the groundwork for your understanding of

Python and prepare you for more complex topics.

Chapter 6-10: We delve into string manipulation, file handling, and data structures. These chapters equip you with the skills to handle real-world data and perform essential operations that are common in many programming tasks.

Chapter 11-15: We explore advanced concepts like object-oriented programming, error handling, and working with APIs. These chapters expand your capabilities and introduce you to more sophisticated programming techniques.

Chapter 16-20: We cover data analysis with Pandas, numerical computations with NumPy, and data visualization with Matplotlib. These chapters are essential for anyone looking to work in data science or related fields.

Chapter 21-25: We delve into network programming, multithreading, unit testing, virtual environments, and deployment. These chapters prepare you for creating robust, scalable, and maintainable applications.

Chapter 26-27: We conclude with advanced Python techniques and working with time and dates, ensuring you have a well-rounded understanding of the language and its capabilities.

Throughout the book, you'll find practical examples, hands-on exercises, and real-world applications that illustrate the concepts and techniques discussed. Our goal is to make learning Python enjoyable and accessible, while also providing the depth and rigor needed to master the language.

Thank you for choosing this book as your guide. Let's embark on this exciting journey together and unlock the full potential of Python programming!

Happy coding!

CHAPTER 1: INTRODUCTION TO PYTHON

1.1 History and Evolution of Python

Python, conceived in the late 1980s by Guido van Rossum, was born out of a need for a better programming language for scripting and automating tasks. Inspired by languages like ABC, Python aimed to balance simplicity and power. Released publicly in 1991, Python has since evolved through numerous versions, each enhancing its capabilities while maintaining its core philosophy: readability and ease of use.

1.2 Key Features and Advantages

Python stands out due to its simple and readable syntax, making it an excellent choice for beginners and seasoned developers alike. Its extensive standard library supports a wide range of tasks from web development to data analysis. Python's cross-platform compatibility ensures that code written on one system runs seamlessly on others. Key features include dynamic typing, automatic memory management, and a robust community that contributes to a vast collection of third-party packages.

1.3 Setting Up the Python Environment

To begin coding in Python, the first step is to set up the development environment:

- **Installation:** Download and install the latest version of Python from the official website (python.org).

- **IDEs and Editors:** Choose an Integrated Development Environment (IDE) or text editor such as PyCharm, VS Code, or Jupyter Notebook, which enhances coding efficiency and offers debugging tools.
- **Environment Variables:** Configure system environment variables to ensure Python can be accessed from the command line.

1.4 Writing and Running Your First Python Program

Let's dive into writing and running your first Python program:

1. **Hello, World!:** Open your chosen editor and create a new file named hello.py. Type the following code:

python
```
print("Hello, World!")
```

2. **Running the Program:** Save the file and open a terminal or command prompt. Navigate to the directory where you saved hello.py and run the command:

bash
```
python hello.py
```

3. **Output:** You should see the output:

4. Hello, World!

Congratulations! You've just written and executed your first Python program. This fundamental exercise sets the stage for more complex and exciting projects as we delve deeper into the world of Python.

CHAPTER 2:
PYTHON BASICS

2.1 Variables and Data Types

Variables are used to store information that can be referenced and manipulated in a program. Python supports several data types:

- **Integers:** Whole numbers (e.g., 5, -3)

python
```
num = 5
```

- **Floats:** Decimal numbers (e.g., 3.14, -0.001)

python
```
pi = 3.14
```

- **Strings:** Text enclosed in quotes (e.g., "Hello", 'Python')

python
```
greeting = "Hello, Python!"
```

- **Booleans:** True or False values

python
```
is_active = True
```

2.2 Basic Operators

Operators are used to perform operations on variables and values:

- **Arithmetic Operators:** + (addition), - (subtraction), * (multiplication), / (division), % (modulus), ** (exponentiation), // (floor division)

python
```
sum = 10 + 5
difference = 10 - 5
product = 10 * 5
quotient = 10 / 5
```

```
remainder = 10 % 3
power = 2 ** 3
floor_div = 10 // 3
```

- **Comparison Operators:** == (equal to), != (not equal to), > (greater than), < (less than), >= (greater than or equal to), <= (less than or equal to)

python
```
equal = 5 == 5
not_equal = 5 != 3
greater = 5 > 3
less = 3 < 5
```

- **Logical Operators:** and, or, not

python
```
result = (5 > 3) and (3 < 5)
```

2.3 Input and Output Functions

Python provides built-in functions to interact with users:

- **Input Function:** input() to take user input

python
```
name = input("Enter your name: ")
```

- **Output Function:** print() to display output

python
```
print("Hello, " + name)
```

2.4 Simple Control Structures

Control structures are used to control the flow of execution in a program:

- **If Statements:** Execute code based on conditions

python
```
if age >= 18:
    print("You are an adult.")
else:
    print("You are a minor.")
```

- **While Loops:** Repeat code while a condition is true

python
```
count = 0
while count < 5:
    print(count)
```

```
count += 1
```

- **For Loops:** Iterate over a sequence (like a list, tuple, or string)

python
```
for i in range(5):
    print(i)
```

This chapter provides the foundational concepts needed to start coding in Python. By understanding variables, data types, operators, and control structures, you will be well-equipped to build more complex programs as you progress through this course.

CHAPTER 3: CONTROL FLOW

3.1 Conditional Statements

Conditional statements allow us to execute code based on certain conditions. The main conditional statements in Python are if, else, and elif.

- **If Statement:** Used to test a specific condition.

python
```
age = 18
if age >= 18:
    print("You are an adult.")
```

- **If-Else Statement:** Provides an alternative block of code if the condition is not met.

python
```
age = 16
if age >= 18:
    print("You are an adult.")
else:
    print("You are a minor.")
```

- **Elif Statement:** Stands for "else if" and allows us to check multiple conditions.

python
```
age = 20
if age < 18:
    print("You are a minor.")
elif age == 18:
    print("You just turned adult!")
else:
    print("You are an adult.")
```

3.2 Loops

Loops are used to execute a block of code repeatedly as long as a condition is true. The main types of loops in Python are while and for loops.

- **While Loop:** Repeats a block of code as long as a condition is true.

python
```python
count = 0
while count < 5:
    print(count)
    count += 1
```

- **For Loop:** Iterates over a sequence (like a list, tuple, or string).

python
```python
for i in range(5):
    print(i)
```

3.3 Break, Continue, and Pass Statements

These statements provide additional control over loops.

- **Break Statement:** Exits the loop prematurely when a certain condition is met.

python
```python
for i in range(10):
    if i == 5:
        break
    print(i)
```

- **Continue Statement:** Skips the current iteration and continues with the next iteration of the loop.

python
```python
for i in range(10):
    if i % 2 == 0:
        continue
    print(i)
```

- **Pass Statement:** A placeholder that does nothing and is used where syntactically required but no action is needed.

python
```
for i in range(5):
    pass
```

3.4 Nested Loops and Conditional Statements

Python allows the use of one or more loops inside another loop, known as nested loops. Similarly, conditional statements can also be nested.

- **Nested Loop:**

python
```
for i in range(3):
    for j in range(2):
        print(f"i = {i}, j = {j}")
```

- **Nested Conditional Statement:**

python
```
num = 5
if num > 0:
    if num % 2 == 0:
        print("Positive and Even")
    else:
        print("Positive and Odd")
else:
    print("Negative or Zero")
```

Understanding control flow is essential for writing efficient and logical programs. Conditional statements and loops are fundamental constructs that enable us to control the sequence and repetition of operations in our code.

CHAPTER 4: FUNCTIONS

4.1 Defining Functions

Functions are reusable blocks of code that perform a specific task. They help in organizing code and reducing redundancy. In Python, functions are defined using the def keyword followed by the function name and parentheses.

- **Syntax:**

python
```
def function_name(parameters):
    # Function body
    return value
```

- **Example:**

python
```
def greet(name):
    return f"Hello, {name}!"

print(greet("Alice"))
```

4.2 Function Arguments and Return Values

Functions can take arguments (parameters) and return values.

- **Positional Arguments:** Passed to a function based on their position.

python
```
def add(a, b):
    return a + b

result = add(5, 3)
print(result)  # Output: 8
```

- **Keyword Arguments:** Passed to a function using the

parameter names.

python
```
def introduce(name, age):
    return f"Name: {name}, Age: {age}"

print(introduce(age=30, name="Bob"))
```

- **Default Arguments:** Have default values if no value is provided.

python
```
def greet(name="Guest"):
    return f"Hello, {name}!"

print(greet()) # Output: Hello, Guest!
print(greet("Alice")) # Output: Hello, Alice!
```

- **Return Values:** Functions can return values using the return statement.

python
```
def square(x):
    return x * x

print(square(4)) # Output: 16
```

4.3 Scope and Lifetime of Variables

The scope of a variable refers to the region of the program where it is accessible. There are two main scopes:

- **Local Scope:** Variables declared inside a function are local and can only be accessed within that function.

python
```
def my_function():
    local_var = 10
    print(local_var)

my_function()
# print(local_var) # This will raise an error
```

- **Global Scope:** Variables declared outside any function are global and can be accessed anywhere in the program.

python
```
global_var = 20

def my_function():
```

```
print(global_var)
```

```
my_function()  # Output: 20
```

4.4 Lambda Functions

Lambda functions are small anonymous functions defined with the lambda keyword. They can have any number of arguments but only one expression.

- **Syntax:**

python
```
lambda arguments: expression
```

- **Example:**

python
```
square = lambda x: x * x
print(square(5))  # Output: 25

add = lambda a, b: a + b
print(add(2, 3))  # Output: 5
```

Functions are fundamental building blocks in Python programming. They allow for code reusability, modularity, and cleaner code organization. Understanding how to define and use functions is essential for writing efficient and maintainable code.

CHAPTER 5: DATA STRUCTURES

5.1 Lists

Lists are ordered collections of items that are mutable. They can hold elements of different data types.

- **Creating Lists:**

python
```
fruits = ["apple", "banana", "cherry"]
```

- **Accessing Elements:**

python
```
print(fruits[0])  # Output: apple
```

- **Modifying Elements:**

python
```
fruits[1] = "blueberry"
```

- **List Methods:**

python
```
fruits.append("date")
fruits.remove("apple")
fruits.sort()
```

5.2 Tuples

Tuples are ordered collections of items that are immutable. Once created, their elements cannot be changed.

- **Creating Tuples:**

python
```
coordinates = (10, 20)
```

- **Accessing Elements:**

python
```
print(coordinates[0]) # Output: 10
```

- **Tuple Methods:** Tuples have fewer methods than lists due to their immutability.

python
```
count = coordinates.count(10)
index = coordinates.index(20)
```

5.3 Dictionaries

Dictionaries are unordered collections of key-value pairs. They are mutable and can hold elements of different data types.

- **Creating Dictionaries:**

python
```
student = {"name": "Alice", "age": 25, "courses": ["Math", "Science"]}
```

- **Accessing Elements:**

python
```
print(student["name"]) # Output: Alice
```

- **Modifying Elements:**

python
```
student["age"] = 26
student["major"] = "Physics"
```

- **Dictionary Methods:**

python
```
keys = student.keys()
values = student.values()
items = student.items()
student.update({"age": 27, "name": "Alicia"})
```

5.4 Sets

Sets are unordered collections of unique elements. They are mutable and typically used for membership testing and eliminating duplicates.

- **Creating Sets:**

python
```
numbers = {1, 2, 3, 4, 5}
```

- **Set Operations:**

python
```
numbers.add(6)
numbers.remove(1)
union_set = numbers.union({7, 8})
intersection_set = numbers.intersection({4, 5, 6})
difference_set = numbers.difference({4, 5})
```

5.5 Comprehensions

Python comprehensions provide a concise way to create lists, dictionaries, and sets.

- **List Comprehensions:**

python
```
squares = [x * x for x in range(10)]
```

- **Dictionary Comprehensions:**

python
```
square_dict = {x: x * x for x in range(10)}
```

- **Set Comprehensions:**

python
```
square_set = {x * x for x in range(10)}
```

CHAPTER 6: STRING MANIPULATION

6.1 Creating and Manipulating Strings

Strings in Python are sequences of characters enclosed in quotes. They can be created using single, double, or triple quotes.

- **Creating Strings:**

```python
single_quote_str = 'Hello'
double_quote_str = "World"
triple_quote_str = """Hello, World!"""
```

- **Accessing Characters:**

```python
sample_str = "Python"
print(sample_str[0]) # Output: P
print(sample_str[-1]) # Output: n
```

- **Slicing Strings:**

```python
print(sample_str[1:4]) # Output: yth
print(sample_str[:3]) # Output: Pyt
print(sample_str[3:]) # Output: hon
```

- **Modifying Strings:** Strings are immutable, so we can't change them directly, but we can create new strings.

```python
modified_str = sample_str.replace("Python", "Java")
print(modified_str) # Output: Java
```

6.2 String Methods

Python provides a rich set of built-in methods to work with strings.

- **Common String Methods:**

python
```
my_str = "Hello, World!"
print(my_str.lower()) # Output: hello, world!
print(my_str.upper()) # Output: HELLO, WORLD!
print(my_str.title()) # Output: Hello, World!
print(my_str.strip()) # Removes whitespace from both ends
print(my_str.find("World")) # Output: 7
print(my_str.replace("World", "Python")) # Output: Hello, Python!
```

6.3 String Formatting

String formatting allows you to create strings with dynamically inserted values.

- **Using Format Method:**

python
```
name = "Alice"
age = 30
greeting = "My name is {} and I am {} years old.".format(name, age)
print(greeting) # Output: My name is Alice and I am 30 years old.
```

- **Using F-Strings (Python 3.6+):**

python
```
greeting = f"My name is {name} and I am {age} years old."
print(greeting) # Output: My name is Alice and I am 30 years old.
```

- **Using Percent (%) Operator:**

python
```
greeting = "My name is %s and I am %d years old." % (name, age)
print(greeting) # Output: My name is Alice and I am 30 years old.
```

6.4 Regular Expressions

Regular expressions (regex) are powerful tools for pattern matching and text manipulation.

- **Importing Regex Module:**

python
```
import re
```

- **Basic Regex Operations:**

python
```
text = "The rain in Spain"
# Search for 'rain'
```

```python
match = re.search(r"rain", text)
if match:
    print("Match found")  # Output: Match found

# Find all occurrences of 'ain'
occurrences = re.findall(r"ain", text)
print(occurrences)  # Output: ['ain', 'ain']

# Substitute 'rain' with 'sun'
replaced_text = re.sub(r"rain", "sun", text)
print(replaced_text)  # Output: The sun in Spain
```

6.5 Working with Unicode

Python supports Unicode, allowing you to work with a wide range of characters and symbols from different languages.

- **Creating Unicode Strings:**

python
```python
unicode_str = u"Hello, \u2764!"
print(unicode_str)  # Output: Hello, ❤!
```

Understanding string manipulation is crucial for processing and analyzing text data. Python provides numerous tools and methods to handle strings efficiently and effectively.

CHAPTER 7: FILE HANDLING

7.1 Introduction to File Handling

File handling is an essential aspect of programming, allowing you to read from and write to files. This chapter will cover the basics of file operations in Python.

7.2 Opening and Closing Files

Files can be opened using the open() function, which returns a file object. The syntax is:

python
```
file_object = open("filename", "mode")
```

- **Modes:**
  - 'r' - Read (default mode)
  - 'w' - Write
  - 'a' - Append
  - 'b' - Binary mode
  - 't' - Text mode (default mode)
- **Example:**

python
```
file = open("example.txt", "r")
# Perform file operations
file.close()
```

- It's a good practice to use the with statement, which ensures that the file is properly closed after its suite finishes, even if an exception is raised:

python

```
with open("example.txt", "r") as file:
    # Perform file operations
    pass
```

7.3 Reading from a File

There are several methods to read the content of a file:

- **Reading the Entire File:**

python
```
with open("example.txt", "r") as file:
    content = file.read()
    print(content)
```

- **Reading Line by Line:**

python
```
with open("example.txt", "r") as file:
    for line in file:
        print(line, end=") # end=" to avoid double newlines
```

- **Reading into a List:**

python
```
with open("example.txt", "r") as file:
    lines = file.readlines()
    print(lines)
```

7.4 Writing to a File

Writing to a file can be done using the write() method. If the file does not exist, it will be created. If it does exist, the content will be overwritten in write mode ('w').

- **Writing Strings:**

python
```
with open("example.txt", "w") as file:
    file.write("Hello, World!\n")
    file.write("Welcome to file handling in Python.")
```

- **Writing Lists:**

python
```
lines = ["Hello, World!\n", "Welcome to file handling in Python.\n"]
with open("example.txt", "w") as file:
    file.writelines(lines)
```

7.5 Appending to a File

Appending to a file can be done using the append mode ('a'). This will add data to the end of the file without overwriting the existing content.

- **Appending Data:**

python
```
with open("example.txt", "a") as file:
    file.write("\nAppending new content to the file.")
```

7.6 Working with File Paths

Python's os module provides functions to work with file paths, making it easier to manage files across different directories and operating systems.

- **Joining Paths:**

python
```
import os
path = os.path.join("folder", "subfolder", "file.txt")
print(path)
```

- **Checking Existence:**

python
```
if os.path.exists("example.txt"):
    print("File exists")
```

- **Getting File Information:**

python
```
info = os.stat("example.txt")
print(f"File size: {info.st_size} bytes")
```

7.7 Handling File Exceptions

Errors can occur during file operations, and it's important to handle them gracefully using try-except blocks.

- **Example:**

python
```
try:
    with open("nonexistent.txt", "r") as file:
        content = file.read()
except FileNotFoundError:
    print("File not found")
except Exception as e:
    print(f"An error occurred: {e}")
```

7.8 File Operations

- **Copying Files:**

python
```
import shutil
shutil.copy("example.txt", "copy_of_example.txt")
```

- **Moving Files:**

python
```
shutil.move("example.txt", "new_location/example.txt")
```

- **Deleting Files:**

python
```
os.remove("example.txt")
```

File handling is a fundamental skill in programming that allows you to manage and manipulate data stored in files. Understanding how to read, write, and handle files efficiently will enhance your ability to work with data in various formats.

CHAPTER 8: MODULES AND PACKAGES

8.1 Introduction to Modules

A module is a file containing Python definitions and statements. Modules allow you to logically organize your Python code, making it easier to manage and reuse.

- **Creating a Module:** Save your code in a file with a .py extension, e.g., mymodule.py.

python
```
# mymodule.py
def greet(name):
    return f"Hello, {name}!"
```

- **Using a Module:** Import the module in another Python script.

python
```
import mymodule
print(mymodule.greet("Alice"))
```

8.2 Importing Modules

Python provides several ways to import modules:

- **Import the Entire Module:**

python
```
import mymodule
print(mymodule.greet("Alice"))
```

- **Import Specific Functions or Variables:**

python
```
from mymodule import greet
print(greet("Bob"))
```

- **Import with an Alias:**

python
```
import mymodule as mm
print(mm.greet("Charlie"))
```

- **Importing Built-in Modules:** Python includes a wide range of built-in modules that can be imported and used in your programs.

python
```
import math
print(math.sqrt(16)) # Output: 4.0
```

8.3 Creating and Using Packages

A package is a way to organize related modules into a single directory. Packages can contain sub-packages and modules.

- **Creating a Package:** Create a directory and add an empty _init_.py file. The directory name becomes the package name.
  - mypackage/
  - _init_.py
  - module1.py
  - module2.py

- **Using a Package:** Import modules from the package.

python
```
from mypackage import module1, module2
print(module1.function1())
print(module2.function2())
```

8.4 Standard Library Overview

Python's standard library includes modules for handling file I/O, system calls, sockets, and much more.

- **Commonly Used Standard Library Modules:**
  - **os:** Interacting with the operating system.

python
```
import os
print(os.getcwd()) # Get current working directory
```

  - **sys:** Access system-specific parameters and functions.

python
```
import sys
print(sys.version) # Get Python version
```

- **datetime:** Working with dates and times.

python
```
from datetime import datetime
print(datetime.now()) # Get current date and time
```

- **random:** Generate pseudo-random numbers.

python
```
import random
print(random.randint(1, 100))  # Random integer between 1 and 100
```

8.5 Installing and Using Third-Party Packages

Python's ecosystem includes a vast collection of third-party packages available through the Python Package Index (PyPI). These packages can be installed using pip.

- **Installing Packages with pip:**

bash
```
pip install requests
```

- **Using Third-Party Packages:**

python
```
import requests
response = requests.get("https://api.example.com/data")
print(response.json())
```

Modules and packages are fundamental concepts in Python that help organize code and reuse functionality. Python's extensive standard library and vibrant ecosystem of third-party packages provide powerful tools to enhance your programs.

CHAPTER 9: ERROR AND EXCEPTION HANDLING

9.1 Types of Errors

Errors in Python can be broadly classified into two categories:

- **Syntax Errors:** These occur when the parser detects an incorrect statement. Syntax errors are usually caused by typos or incorrect usage of Python syntax.

python
```
print("Hello, World"  # SyntaxError: Missing closing parenthesis
```

- **Exceptions:** These are errors that occur during the execution of a program. Exceptions can be caused by various reasons like invalid user input, file not found, or division by zero.

python
```
number = 10 / 0  # ZeroDivisionError
```

9.2 Handling Exceptions

Python provides a way to handle exceptions using the try, except, else, and finally blocks.

- **Try and Except Block:**

python
```
try:
    numerator = int(input("Enter numerator: "))
    denominator = int(input("Enter denominator: "))
    result = numerator / denominator
    print(f"Result: {result}")
```

```python
except ZeroDivisionError:
    print("Error: Division by zero is not allowed.")
except ValueError:
    print("Error: Invalid input. Please enter a number.")
```

- **Else Block:** The else block is executed if no exceptions are raised in the try block.

python
```python
try:
    file = open("example.txt", "r")
except FileNotFoundError:
    print("Error: File not found.")
else:
    content = file.read()
    print(content)
    file.close()
```

- **Finally Block:** The finally block is executed no matter what, even if an exception is raised. It is generally used for cleanup actions like closing files or releasing resources.

python
```python
try:
    file = open("example.txt", "r")
except FileNotFoundError:
    print("Error: File not found.")
else:
    content = file.read()
    print(content)
finally:
    file.close()
```

9.3 Catching Multiple Exceptions

You can handle multiple exceptions by specifying them in a tuple or using multiple except blocks.

- **Catching Multiple Exceptions in a Tuple:**

python
```python
try:
    numerator = int(input("Enter numerator: "))
    denominator = int(input("Enter denominator: "))
    result = numerator / denominator
    print(f"Result: {result}")
```

```
except (ZeroDivisionError, ValueError) as e:
    print(f"Error: {e}")
```

- **Using Multiple Except Blocks:**

python
```
try:
    numerator = int(input("Enter numerator: "))
    denominator = int(input("Enter denominator: "))
    result = numerator / denominator
    print(f"Result: {result}")
except ZeroDivisionError:
    print("Error: Division by zero is not allowed.")
except ValueError:
    print("Error: Invalid input. Please enter a number.")
```

9.4 Raising Exceptions

You can raise exceptions using the raise keyword.

- **Raising an Exception:**

python
```
def check_age(age):
    if age < 0:
        raise ValueError("Age cannot be negative.")
    return f"Age is {age}."

try:
    print(check_age(-1))
except ValueError as e:
    print(f"Error: {e}")
```

9.5 Custom Exceptions

You can define custom exceptions by creating a new class that inherits from the built-in Exception class.

- **Defining a Custom Exception:**

python
```
class CustomError(Exception):
    def __init__(self, message):
        self.message = message
        super().__init__(self.message)

try:
    raise CustomError("This is a custom error message.")
except CustomError as e:
    print(f"Error: {e}")
```

9.6 Debugging Techniques

Debugging is the process of identifying and removing errors from your code. Python provides several tools and techniques for debugging:

- **Print Statements:** Use print statements to display variable values and program flow.

python
```
x = 5
print(f"x = {x}")
```

- **Using Assertions:** Assertions are used to check if a condition is true during development. If the condition is false, an AssertionError is raised.

python
```
assert x == 5, "x should be 5"
```

- **Using a Debugger:** Python provides a built-in debugger module called pdb.

python
```
import pdb
pdb.set_trace()
```

Error and exception handling are crucial for building robust and reliable programs. By effectively handling errors, you can ensure that your programs can gracefully recover from unexpected situations and continue to function as intended.

CHAPTER 10: OBJECT-ORIENTED PROGRAMMING (OOP)

10.1 Introduction to Object-Oriented Programming

Object-Oriented Programming (OOP) is a programming paradigm that uses objects and classes to structure code. It enables developers to create modular, reusable, and maintainable software. Key concepts in OOP include classes, objects, inheritance, polymorphism, encapsulation, and abstraction.

10.2 Classes and Objects

Classes are blueprints for creating objects, defining the properties and behaviors that the objects will have. Objects are instances of classes.

- **Defining a Class:**

python
```
class Animal:
    def __init__(self, name):
        self.name = name

    def speak(self):
        pass
```

- **Creating an Object:**

python
```
class Dog(Animal):
    def speak(self):
        return f"{self.name} says Woof!"

class Cat(Animal):
```

```python
    def speak(self):
        return f"{self.name} says Meow!"

my_dog = Dog("Buddy")
my_cat = Cat("Whiskers")

print(my_dog.speak())  # Output: Buddy says Woof!
print(my_cat.speak())  # Output: Whiskers says Meow!
```

10.3 Inheritance

Inheritance allows a class to inherit attributes and methods from another class, promoting code reuse and organization.

- **Base and Derived Classes:**

python
```python
class Animal:
    def __init__(self, name):
        self.name = name

    def speak(self):
        pass

class Dog(Animal):
    def speak(self):
        return f"{self.name} says Woof!"

class Cat(Animal):
    def speak(self):
        return f"{self.name} says Meow!"
```

- **Creating Derived Objects:**

python
```python
my_dog = Dog("Buddy")
my_cat = Cat("Whiskers")

print(my_dog.speak())  # Output: Buddy says Woof!
print(my_cat.speak())  # Output: Whiskers says Meow!
```

10.4 Polymorphism

Polymorphism allows different classes to be treated as instances of the same class through a common interface. It enables functions to use objects of different types.

- **Polymorphic Behavior:**

python
```python
def animal_speak(animal):
```

```
    print(animal.speak())

my_dog = Dog("Buddy")
my_cat = Cat("Whiskers")

animal_speak(my_dog)  # Output: Buddy says Woof!
animal_speak(my_cat)  # Output: Whiskers says Meow!
```

10.5 Encapsulation and Abstraction

Encapsulation is the practice of keeping data and methods that operate on the data within a single unit (class). Abstraction is the concept of hiding the complex implementation details and showing only the necessary features.

- **Encapsulation:**

python
```
class Account:
    def __init__(self, owner, balance):
        self.owner = owner
        self.__balance = balance  # Private attribute

    def deposit(self, amount):
        self.__balance += amount

    def withdraw(self, amount):
        if amount <= self.__balance:
            self.__balance -= amount
            return True
        else:
            return False

    def get_balance(self):
        return self.__balance
```

- **Abstraction:**

python
```
class Shape:
    def area(self):
        pass

class Rectangle(Shape):
    def __init__(self, width, height):
        self.width = width
        self.height = height

    def area(self):
```

```
        return self.width * self.height

class Circle(Shape):
    def __init__(self, radius):
        self.radius = radius

    def area(self):
        return 3.14 * (self.radius ** 2)

rect = Rectangle(4, 5)
circ = Circle(3)

print(rect.area())  # Output: 20
print(circ.area())  # Output: 28.26
```

Object-Oriented Programming in Python provides a robust and flexible way to build programs. By understanding and utilizing OOP principles, you can write code that is more modular, reusable, and easier to maintain.

CHAPTER 11: ADVANCED OOP CONCEPTS

11.1 Class Methods and Static Methods

In addition to regular instance methods, Python supports class methods and static methods, which are defined using the @classmethod and @staticmethod decorators, respectively.

- **Class Methods:** Class methods receive the class as the first argument and can modify class-level attributes.

python
```python
class Dog:
    species = "Canis lupus familiaris"

    def __init__(self, name):
        self.name = name

    @classmethod
    def get_species(cls):
        return cls.species

print(Dog.get_species())  # Output: Canis lupus familiaris
```

- **Static Methods:** Static methods do not receive an implicit first argument and behave like regular functions but belong to the class's namespace.

python
```python
class Math:
    @staticmethod
    def add(a, b):
        return a + b
```

```
print(Math.add(5, 3)) # Output: 8
```

11.2 Magic Methods and Operator Overloading

Magic methods (also known as dunder methods) allow you to define the behavior of objects for built-in operations like arithmetic, comparison, and string representation.

- **Common Magic Methods:**

python
```python
class Vector:
    def __init__(self, x, y):
        self.x = x
        self.y = y

    def __add__(self, other):
        return Vector(self.x + other.x, self.y + other.y)

    def __str__(self):
        return f"({self.x}, {self.y})"

v1 = Vector(2, 3)
v2 = Vector(4, 5)
v3 = v1 + v2
print(v3) # Output: (6, 8)
```

11.3 Composition and Aggregation

Composition and aggregation are design principles used to build complex objects from simpler ones. They are similar concepts, but with key differences.

- **Composition:** In composition, the contained objects do not exist independently of the container object.

python
```python
class Engine:
    def __init__(self, horsepower):
        self.horsepower = horsepower

class Car:
    def __init__(self, model, engine):
        self.model = model
        self.engine = engine # Composition

engine = Engine(200)
car = Car("Toyota", engine)
```

```python
print(car.engine.horsepower) # Output: 200
```

- **Aggregation:** In aggregation, the contained objects can exist independently of the container object.

python
```python
class Book:
    def __init__(self, title):
        self.title = title

class Library:
    def __init__(self):
        self.books = [] # Aggregation

    def add_book(self, book):
        self.books.append(book)

book1 = Book("1984")
book2 = Book("Animal Farm")
library = Library()
library.add_book(book1)
library.add_book(book2)
print([book.title for book in library.books])  # Output: ['1984', 'Animal Farm']
```

11.4 Mixins and Multiple Inheritance

Mixins are a way to provide additional functionality to classes through multiple inheritance without forming a complex class hierarchy.

- **Using Mixins:**

python
```python
class WalkMixin:
    def walk(self):
        return "Walking"

class TalkMixin:
    def talk(self):
        return "Talking"

class Robot(WalkMixin, TalkMixin):
    pass

r = Robot()
print(r.walk()) # Output: Walking
print(r.talk()) # Output: Talking
```

- **Multiple Inheritance:** Multiple inheritance allows a class to inherit from multiple base classes, allowing for more flexible designs.

python
```python
class Animal:
    def eat(self):
        return "Eating"

class Bird(Animal):
    def fly(self):
        return "Flying"

class Parrot(Bird):
    def speak(self):
        return "Speaking"

parrot = Parrot()
print(parrot.eat())   # Output: Eating
print(parrot.fly())   # Output: Flying
print(parrot.speak()) # Output: Speaking
```

Advanced OOP concepts such as class methods, static methods, magic methods, operator overloading, composition, aggregation, mixins, and multiple inheritance provide powerful tools for designing and building flexible, reusable, and maintainable software systems.

CHAPTER 12: PYTHON STANDARD LIBRARIES

12.1 Introduction to Python Standard Libraries

Python's standard library is a collection of modules and packages that come bundled with Python, offering a wide range of functionalities. These libraries eliminate the need to write common functions from scratch and provide a consistent and reliable set of tools for various tasks.

12.2 OS and SYS Modules

- **OS Module:** The os module provides a way to interact with the operating system. It includes functions for file and directory manipulation, process management, and environment variables.

python
```
import os
print(os.getcwd()) # Get current working directory
os.mkdir("new_folder") # Create a new directory
os.rename("old_name.txt", "new_name.txt") # Rename a file
os.remove("file_to_delete.txt") # Delete a file
```

- **SYS Module:** The sys module provides access to system-specific parameters and functions. It includes functions to manipulate the Python runtime environment.

python
```
import sys
print(sys.version) # Get Python version
sys.exit() # Exit the program
print(sys.argv) # Get command-line arguments
```

12.3 Date and Time Manipulation

The datetime module supplies classes for manipulating dates and times. It supports arithmetic operations on dates and times and provides various formatting options.

python
```
from datetime import datetime, timedelta

# Get current date and time
now = datetime.now()
print(now)

# Format date and time
formatted_date = now.strftime("%Y-%m-%d %H:%M:%S")
print(formatted_date)

# Parse a string into a datetime object
date_str = "2023-12-21 20:00:00"
parsed_date = datetime.strptime(date_str, "%Y-%m-%d %H:%M:%S")
print(parsed_date)

# Date arithmetic
future_date = now + timedelta(days=10)
print(future_date)
```

12.4 Math and Statistics Modules

Python's math and statistics modules provide mathematical functions and statistical operations, respectively.

- **Math Module:**

python
```
import math
print(math.sqrt(16)) # Output: 4.0
print(math.factorial(5)) # Output: 120
print(math.pi) # Output: 3.141592653589793
```

- **Statistics Module:**

python
```
import statistics
data = [1, 2, 3, 4, 5]
print(statistics.mean(data)) # Output: 3
print(statistics.median(data)) # Output: 3
print(statistics.variance(data)) # Output: 2.5
```

12.5 Collections Module

The collections module provides specialized container datatypes that extend the capabilities of Python's built-in types.

- **Named Tuple:** A tuple with named fields.

python
```
from collections import namedtuple
Point = namedtuple("Point", ["x", "y"])
p = Point(10, 20)
print(p.x, p.y) # Output: 10 20
```

- **Deque:** A double-ended queue that supports adding and removing elements from both ends.

python
```
from collections import deque
d = deque([1, 2, 3])
d.append(4)
d.appendleft(0)
print(d) # Output: deque([0, 1, 2, 3, 4])
d.pop()
d.popleft()
print(d) # Output: deque([1, 2, 3])
```

- **Counter:** A dictionary subclass for counting hashable objects.

python
```
from collections import Counter
counts = Counter(["a", "b", "a", "c", "a", "b"])
print(counts) # Output: Counter({'a': 3, 'b': 2, 'c': 1})
```

- **OrderedDict:** A dictionary subclass that preserves the order of items.

python
```
from collections import OrderedDict
od = OrderedDict()
od["one"] = 1
od["two"] = 2
od["three"] = 3
print(od) # Output: OrderedDict([('one', 1), ('two', 2), ('three', 3)])
```

Python's standard libraries provide a wealth of functionality that can simplify many programming tasks. By leveraging these libraries, you can write more efficient, reliable, and maintainable code.

CHAPTER 13: WORKING WITH JSON AND CSV

13.1 Introduction to JSON

JSON (JavaScript Object Notation) is a lightweight data interchange format that is easy for humans to read and write, and easy for machines to parse and generate. It is commonly used for transmitting data in web applications.

- **JSON Structure:**

```json
json
{
    "name": "John",
    "age": 30,
    "city": "New York"
}
```

13.2 Reading and Writing JSON Data

Python provides built-in support for working with JSON data through the json module.

- **Reading JSON Data:**

```python
python
import json

json_data = '{"name": "John", "age": 30, "city": "New York"}'
data = json.loads(json_data)
print(data["name"])  # Output: John
```

- **Writing JSON Data:**

```python
python
```

```
import json

data = {
    "name": "John",
    "age": 30,
    "city": "New York"
}
json_data = json.dumps(data)
print(json_data)  # Output: {"name": "John", "age": 30, "city": "New York"}
```

- **Reading from a JSON File:**

python
```
import json

with open('data.json', 'r') as file:
    data = json.load(file)
print(data)
```

- **Writing to a JSON File:**

python
```
import json

data = {
    "name": "John",
    "age": 30,
    "city": "New York"
}
with open('data.json', 'w') as file:
    json.dump(data, file)
```

13.3 Parsing and Generating JSON

JSON data can be parsed (converted to Python objects) and generated (converted to JSON format) using the json module.

- **Parsing JSON Data:**

python
```
import json

json_data = '{"name": "John", "age": 30, "city": "New York"}'
data = json.loads(json_data)
```

- **Generating JSON Data:**

python
```
import json

data = {
```

```
    "name": "John",
    "age": 30,
    "city": "New York"
}
json_data = json.dumps(data)
```

13.4 Introduction to CSV

CSV (Comma Separated Values) is a simple file format used to store tabular data, such as a spreadsheet or database. Each line of the file is a data record, and each record consists of one or more fields separated by commas.

- **CSV Structure:**

```csv
csv
name,age,city
John,30,New York
Jane,25,Los Angeles
```

13.5 Reading and Writing CSV Files

Python provides the csv module to work with CSV files.

- **Reading CSV Files:**

```python
python
import csv

with open('data.csv', 'r') as file:
    csv_reader = csv.reader(file)
    for row in csv_reader:
        print(row)
```

- **Writing CSV Files:**

```python
python
import csv

data = [
    ["name", "age", "city"],
    ["John", 30, "New York"],
    ["Jane", 25, "Los Angeles"]
]
with open('data.csv', 'w', newline='') as file:
    csv_writer = csv.writer(file)
    csv_writer.writerows(data)
```

13.6 CSV File Operations

CSV files can also be read and written using dictionaries, which can be more convenient for working with named fields.

- **Reading CSV Files with DictReader:**

python
```
import csv

with open('data.csv', 'r') as file:
    csv_reader = csv.DictReader(file)
    for row in csv_reader:
        print(row)
```

- **Writing CSV Files with DictWriter:**

python
```
import csv

data = [
    {"name": "John", "age": 30, "city": "New York"},
    {"name": "Jane", "age": 25, "city": "Los Angeles"}
]
with open('data.csv', 'w', newline='') as file:
    fieldnames = ["name", "age", "city"]
    csv_writer = csv.DictWriter(file, fieldnames=fieldnames)
    csv_writer.writeheader()
    csv_writer.writerows(data)
```

Working with JSON and CSV files is essential for data manipulation and exchange in Python. These formats are widely used in web applications, data processing, and machine learning, making it crucial to understand how to read, write, and handle them effectively.

CHAPTER 14: WEB SCRAPING

14.1 Introduction to Web Scraping

Web scraping is the process of extracting data from websites. It involves retrieving web pages and extracting specific information for various purposes such as data analysis, research, and automation. While web scraping can be powerful, it's important to adhere to legal and ethical guidelines, such as respecting a website's terms of service and using scraping techniques responsibly.

14.2 Using Requests for Web Scraping

The requests library in Python is used to send HTTP requests to web servers and receive responses. It is often the first step in web scraping, as it allows you to fetch the raw HTML content of web pages.

- **Installing Requests:**

bash
```
pip install requests
```

- **Fetching a Web Page:**

python
```
import requests

url = "https://example.com"
response = requests.get(url)

if response.status_code == 200:
    html_content = response.text
    print(html_content)
else:
```

```
print("Failed to retrieve the web page.")
```

14.3 Parsing HTML with BeautifulSoup

BeautifulSoup is a Python library used for parsing HTML and XML documents. It provides idiomatic ways to navigate, search, and modify the parse tree.

- **Installing BeautifulSoup:**

bash
```
pip install beautifulsoup4
```

- **Parsing HTML Content:**

python
```
from bs4 import BeautifulSoup

html_content = "<html><body><h1>Hello, World!</h1></body></html>"
soup = BeautifulSoup(html_content, "html.parser")
print(soup.prettify())
```

- **Extracting Data:**

python
```
from bs4 import BeautifulSoup
import requests

url = "https://example.com"
response = requests.get(url)
soup = BeautifulSoup(response.text, "html.parser")

title = soup.title.text
print(title)

headings = soup.find_all('h1')
for heading in headings:
    print(heading.text)
```

14.4 Handling AJAX and JavaScript with Selenium

Some websites use JavaScript to dynamically load content, making it difficult to scrape using just requests and BeautifulSoup. Selenium is a powerful tool that automates web browsers and can be used to interact with JavaScript-heavy websites.

- **Installing Selenium:**

bash
```
pip install selenium
```

- **Setting Up WebDriver:**

python
```
from selenium import webdriver
from selenium.webdriver.common.by import By

driver = webdriver.Chrome(executable_path='/path/to/chromedriver')
driver.get("https://example.com")

title = driver.title
print(title)

heading = driver.find_element(By.TAG_NAME, 'h1').text
print(heading)

driver.quit()
```

14.5 Ethical Considerations in Web Scraping

Web scraping should be done responsibly and ethically. Here are some best practices to follow:

- **Respect Robots.txt:** Check the robots.txt file of the website to see if web scraping is allowed and to understand the rules set by the website.

python
```
url = "https://example.com/robots.txt"
response = requests.get(url)
print(response.text)
```

- **Avoid Overloading Servers:** Send requests at reasonable intervals to avoid putting undue load on the web server.
- **Use User-Agent Strings:** Identify your requests by setting a user-agent string that informs the server about the source of the requests.

python
```
headers = {"User-Agent": "Mozilla/5.0 (compatible; Web Scraper/1.0)"}
response = requests.get(url, headers=headers)
```

- **Legal and Privacy Concerns:** Ensure that your web scraping activities comply with legal and privacy regulations. Do not scrape personal data or use the data for malicious purposes.

Web scraping is a valuable skill for extracting data from the web, but it must be performed responsibly and ethically. By using tools like requests, BeautifulSoup, and Selenium, you can effectively scrape and process web data for various applications.

CHAPTER 15:
WORKING WITH APIS

15.1 Introduction to APIs

An API (Application Programming Interface) allows different software applications to communicate with each other. APIs are used to request and exchange data between systems. They can be public or private and can range from simple data retrieval to complex operations.

15.2 Understanding APIs

APIs typically use HTTP protocols to send requests and receive responses. Each request consists of:

- **Endpoint:** The URL of the API.
- **Method:** The type of request (GET, POST, PUT, DELETE).
- **Headers:** Metadata about the request (e.g., authentication tokens).
- **Body:** Data sent with the request (for POST and PUT methods).

15.3 Making API Requests with Requests

Python's requests library simplifies the process of making HTTP requests.

- **Installing Requests:**

bash
```
pip install requests
```

- **GET Request:**

python
```
import requests
```

```python
url = "https://api.example.com/data"
response = requests.get(url)

if response.status_code == 200:
    data = response.json() # Parsing JSON response
    print(data)
else:
    print("Failed to retrieve data.")
```

- **POST Request:**

python
```python
import requests

url = "https://api.example.com/data"
payload = {"key1": "value1", "key2": "value2"}
headers = {"Content-Type": "application/json"}

response = requests.post(url, json=payload, headers=headers)

if response.status_code == 201:
    data = response.json()
    print(data)
else:
    print("Failed to create data.")
```

15.4 Parsing API Responses

API responses are typically in JSON format, which can be parsed into Python dictionaries or lists for easy manipulation.

- **Parsing JSON Response:**

python
```python
response = requests.get("https://api.example.com/data")
data = response.json()
print(data["key"])
```

15.5 Handling API Errors and Rate Limits

API requests can fail for various reasons such as network issues, invalid requests, or server errors. It's important to handle these errors gracefully.

- **Error Handling:**

python
```python
response = requests.get("https://api.example.com/data")

if response.status_code == 200:
```

```
    data = response.json()
elif response.status_code == 404:
    print("Resource not found.")
else:
    print("An error occurred:", response.status_code)
```

- **Rate Limits:** Some APIs enforce rate limits to control the number of requests a user can make. Handling rate limits involves checking the response headers and implementing delays or retries.

python
```
import time
response = requests.get("https://api.example.com/data")

if response.status_code == 429:  # Too Many Requests
    retry_after = int(response.headers.get("Retry-After", 60))
    time.sleep(retry_after)
    response = requests.get("https://api.example.com/data")
```

15.6 Authenticating API Requests

Many APIs require authentication to access data. Common authentication methods include API keys, OAuth tokens, and Basic Authentication.

- **Using API Keys:**

python
```
api_key = "your_api_key"
headers = {"Authorization": f"Bearer {api_key}"}
response          =          requests.get("https://api.example.com/data",
headers=headers)
```

- **OAuth Tokens:**

python
```
token = "your_oauth_token"
headers = {"Authorization": f"Bearer {token}"}
response          =          requests.get("https://api.example.com/data",
headers=headers)
```

- **Basic Authentication:**

python
```
from requests.auth import HTTPBasicAuth

response          =          requests.get("https://api.example.com/data",
auth=HTTPBasicAuth("username", "password"))
```

15.7 Best Practices for Working with APIs

- **Read API Documentation:** Understand the available endpoints, methods, and data formats.

- **Handle Errors Gracefully:** Implement robust error handling to manage different response statuses.

- **Rate Limiting:** Respect the rate limits set by the API provider to avoid being blocked.

- **Secure Authentication:** Keep your API keys and tokens secure. Avoid hardcoding them in your source code.

- **Optimize Requests:** Minimize the number of API calls to reduce latency and improve performance.

Working with APIs is essential for integrating different systems and accessing external data. By understanding how to make requests, parse responses, handle errors, and authenticate, you can effectively interact with APIs in your applications.

CHAPTER 16: DATA ANALYSIS WITH PANDAS

16.1 Introduction to Pandas

Pandas is a powerful and flexible open-source data analysis and manipulation library for Python. It provides data structures like DataFrames and Series, which are essential for handling and analyzing structured data.

- **Installing Pandas:**

bash
```
pip install pandas
```

16.2 DataFrames and Series

- **Series:** A one-dimensional labeled array capable of holding any data type.

python
```
import pandas as pd

data = [1, 2, 3, 4, 5]
series = pd.Series(data)
print(series)
```

- **DataFrame:** A two-dimensional labeled data structure with columns of potentially different types.

python
```
import pandas as pd

data = {
    "Name": ["Alice", "Bob", "Charlie"],
    "Age": [25, 30, 35],
```

```
        "City": ["New York", "Los Angeles", "Chicago"]
    }
    df = pd.DataFrame(data)
    print(df)
```

16.3 Data Cleaning

Data cleaning involves preparing and correcting data to ensure it is accurate and usable for analysis.

- **Handling Missing Data:**

python
```
df = pd.DataFrame({
    "Name": ["Alice", "Bob", None],
    "Age": [25, None, 35],
    "City": ["New York", None, "Chicago"]
})
# Drop rows with missing values
df_cleaned = df.dropna()
# Fill missing values
df_filled = df.fillna({"Name": "Unknown", "Age": 0, "City": "Unknown"})
print(df_cleaned)
print(df_filled)
```

- **Removing Duplicates:**

python
```
df = pd.DataFrame({
    "Name": ["Alice", "Bob", "Alice"],
    "Age": [25, 30, 25],
    "City": ["New York", "Los Angeles", "New York"]
})
df_no_duplicates = df.drop_duplicates()
print(df_no_duplicates)
```

16.4 Data Transformation

Data transformation involves converting data into a suitable format for analysis.

- **Renaming Columns:**

python
```
df = pd.DataFrame({
    "Name": ["Alice", "Bob", "Charlie"],
    "Age": [25, 30, 35],
    "City": ["New York", "Los Angeles", "Chicago"]
})
```

```python
df_renamed = df.rename(columns={"Name": "Full Name", "Age": "Years"})
print(df_renamed)
```

- **Applying Functions:**

```python
python
df = pd.DataFrame({
    "Name": ["Alice", "Bob", "Charlie"],
    "Age": [25, 30, 35],
    "City": ["New York", "Los Angeles", "Chicago"]
})
df["Age in Months"] = df["Age"].apply(lambda x: x * 12)
print(df)
```

16.5 Data Aggregation and Grouping

Data aggregation involves summarizing data, and grouping involves splitting data into subsets.

- **Grouping and Aggregating:**

```python
python
df = pd.DataFrame({
    "Name": ["Alice", "Bob", "Charlie", "David"],
    "Age": [25, 30, 35, 40],
    "City": ["New York", "Los Angeles", "New York", "Chicago"]
})
grouped = df.groupby("City")
age_summary = grouped["Age"].agg(["mean", "min", "max"])
print(age_summary)
```

16.6 Data Visualization with Pandas

Pandas integrates well with data visualization libraries like Matplotlib and Seaborn to create plots directly from DataFrames.

- **Plotting Data:**

```python
python
import pandas as pd
import matplotlib.pyplot as plt

df = pd.DataFrame({
    "Month": ["January", "February", "March"],
    "Sales": [250, 300, 400]
})
df.plot(kind="bar", x="Month", y="Sales", legend=False)
plt.title("Monthly Sales")
plt.xlabel("Month")
```

```
plt.ylabel("Sales")
plt.show()
```

Data analysis with Pandas provides a powerful toolkit for handling, cleaning, transforming, and visualizing data. By mastering Pandas, you can perform sophisticated data analysis tasks with ease and efficiency.

CHAPTER 17: NUMPY FOR NUMERICAL COMPUTATIONS

17.1 Introduction to NumPy

NumPy (Numerical Python) is a powerful library for numerical computing in Python. It provides support for arrays, matrices, and many mathematical functions to operate on these data structures efficiently.

- **Installing NumPy:**

bash
```
pip install numpy
```

17.2 Arrays and Array Operations

NumPy arrays are the core data structure provided by the library. They are more efficient than Python lists for numerical computations.

- **Creating Arrays:**

python
```
import numpy as np

# Creating a one-dimensional array
arr1 = np.array([1, 2, 3, 4, 5])

# Creating a two-dimensional array
arr2 = np.array([[1, 2, 3], [4, 5, 6]])

# Creating an array with a range of numbers
arr3 = np.arange(10)

# Creating an array with evenly spaced numbers
```

```python
arr4 = np.linspace(0, 1, 5)
```

- **Basic Array Operations:**

python
```python
arr = np.array([1, 2, 3, 4, 5])

# Element-wise operations
arr2 = arr + 10
arr3 = arr * 2

# Aggregation operations
sum_arr = np.sum(arr)
mean_arr = np.mean(arr)
```

- **Indexing and Slicing:**

python
```python
arr = np.array([1, 2, 3, 4, 5])

# Indexing
print(arr[0]) # Output: 1

# Slicing
print(arr[1:4]) # Output: [2 3 4]
```

17.3 Mathematical Functions with NumPy

NumPy provides a wide range of mathematical functions to perform operations on arrays.

- **Common Mathematical Functions:**

python
```python
arr = np.array([1, 2, 3, 4, 5])

sqrt_arr = np.sqrt(arr)
exp_arr = np.exp(arr)
sin_arr = np.sin(arr)
log_arr = np.log(arr)
```

17.4 Linear Algebra with NumPy

NumPy includes functions to perform linear algebra operations on matrices and arrays.

- **Matrix Operations:**

python
```python
A = np.array([[1, 2], [3, 4]])
B = np.array([[5, 6], [7, 8]])
```

```
# Matrix addition
C = A + B

# Matrix multiplication
D = np.dot(A, B)

# Determinant of a matrix
det_A = np.linalg.det(A)

# Inverse of a matrix
inv_A = np.linalg.inv(A)
```

17.5 Random Number Generation with NumPy

NumPy provides functions to generate random numbers for various distributions.

- **Generating Random Numbers:**

python
```
# Random numbers from a uniform distribution
rand_arr = np.random.rand(5)

# Random numbers from a normal distribution
normal_arr = np.random.randn(5)

# Random integers
int_arr = np.random.randint(0, 10, size=5)
```

17.6 Handling Missing Data with NumPy

NumPy can handle missing data using special values like NaN (Not a Number).

- **Handling Missing Data:**

python
```
arr = np.array([1, 2, np.nan, 4, 5])

# Check for NaN values
is_nan = np.isnan(arr)

# Replace NaN values
arr_cleaned = np.nan_to_num(arr, nan=0)
```

NumPy is a fundamental library for numerical computations in Python. Its efficient array operations, mathematical functions, and support for linear algebra and random number generation make it an indispensable tool for data analysis and scientific computing.

CHAPTER 18: DATA VISUALIZATION WITH MATPLOTLIB

18.1 Introduction to Data Visualization

Data visualization is the graphical representation of information and data. By using visual elements like charts, graphs, and maps, data visualization tools provide an accessible way to see and understand trends, outliers, and patterns in data.

18.2 Introduction to Matplotlib

Matplotlib is a comprehensive library for creating static, animated, and interactive visualizations in Python. It is highly customizable and can produce publication-quality figures.

- **Installing Matplotlib:**

bash
```
pip install matplotlib
```

18.3 Basic Plotting with Matplotlib

- **Creating a Simple Line Plot:**

python
```
import matplotlib.pyplot as plt

x = [1, 2, 3, 4, 5]
y = [2, 3, 5, 7, 11]

plt.plot(x, y)
plt.xlabel("X Axis")
plt.ylabel("Y Axis")
plt.title("Simple Line Plot")
plt.show()
```

- **Customizing Plots:**

```python
plt.plot(x, y, color='red', linestyle='--', marker='o')
plt.xlabel("X Axis")
plt.ylabel("Y Axis")
plt.title("Customized Line Plot")
plt.grid(True)
plt.show()
```

18.4 Types of Plots

Matplotlib supports a variety of plot types for different visualization needs.

- **Bar Plot:**

```python
categories = ["A", "B", "C", "D"]
values = [10, 20, 15, 25]

plt.bar(categories, values, color='blue')
plt.xlabel("Categories")
plt.ylabel("Values")
plt.title("Bar Plot")
plt.show()
```

- **Histogram:**

```python
data = [1, 2, 2, 3, 3, 3, 4, 4, 5]

plt.hist(data, bins=5, color='green')
plt.xlabel("Data Bins")
plt.ylabel("Frequency")
plt.title("Histogram")
plt.show()
```

- **Scatter Plot:**

```python
x = [1, 2, 3, 4, 5]
y = [2, 3, 5, 7, 11]

plt.scatter(x, y, color='purple')
plt.xlabel("X Axis")
plt.ylabel("Y Axis")
plt.title("Scatter Plot")
plt.show()
```

- **Pie Chart:**

python
```
sizes = [15, 30, 45, 10]
labels = ["A", "B", "C", "D"]
colors = ["gold", "yellowgreen", "lightcoral", "lightskyblue"]
explode = (0.1, 0, 0, 0)  # explode the 1st slice

plt.pie(sizes, explode=explode, labels=labels, colors=colors,
autopct='%1.1f%%', shadow=True, startangle=140)
plt.title("Pie Chart")
plt.show()
```

18.5 Customizing Plots

Matplotlib provides extensive customization options to enhance the appearance of plots.

- **Adding Legends:**

python
```
plt.plot(x, y, label='Line 1')
plt.plot([1, 2, 3, 4, 5], [1, 4, 9, 16, 25], label='Line 2')
plt.xlabel("X Axis")
plt.ylabel("Y Axis")
plt.title("Plot with Legends")
plt.legend()
plt.show()
```

- **Subplots:**

python
```
fig, axs = plt.subplots(2, 1, figsize=(5, 10))

axs[0].plot(x, y, color='red')
axs[0].set_title("Subplot 1")

axs[1].plot([1, 2, 3, 4, 5], [1, 4, 9, 16, 25], color='blue')
axs[1].set_title("Subplot 2")

plt.tight_layout()
plt.show()
```

18.6 Advanced Customization

Matplotlib allows for advanced customization to create professional-quality visualizations.

- **Setting Axis Limits:**

python
```
plt.plot(x, y)
plt.xlim(0, 6)
plt.ylim(0, 12)
plt.xlabel("X Axis")
plt.ylabel("Y Axis")
plt.title("Plot with Axis Limits")
plt.show()
```

- **Annotating Plots:**

python
```
plt.plot(x, y)
plt.annotate('Max    Value',    xy=(5,    11),    xytext=(3,    10),
arrowprops=dict(facecolor='black', shrink=0.05))
plt.xlabel("X Axis")
plt.ylabel("Y Axis")
plt.title("Annotated Plot")
plt.show()
```

18.7 Saving Plots

Matplotlib allows you to save plots in various formats, including PNG, PDF, and SVG.

- **Saving a Plot:**

python
```
plt.plot(x, y)
plt.xlabel("X Axis")
plt.ylabel("Y Axis")
plt.title("Save Plot Example")
plt.savefig("plot.png")
plt.show()
```

Data visualization with Matplotlib empowers you to create clear and informative visual representations of your data. Mastering the customization and advanced features of Matplotlib will enable you to convey insights effectively through your visualizations.

CHAPTER 19:
DATABASES AND SQL

19.1 Introduction to Databases

Databases are organized collections of data that can be easily accessed, managed, and updated. They are essential for storing and retrieving large amounts of structured data efficiently. Common database management systems (DBMS) include SQLite, MySQL, PostgreSQL, and SQL Server.

19.2 Introduction to SQL

SQL (Structured Query Language) is a standardized language used to manage and manipulate relational databases. It provides commands for querying, updating, and managing data.

- **Basic SQL Commands:**
  - **SELECT:** Retrieve data from a database.
  - **INSERT:** Add new data to a database.
  - **UPDATE:** Modify existing data in a database.
  - **DELETE:** Remove data from a database.

19.3 Connecting Python with Databases using SQLite

SQLite is a lightweight, self-contained database engine that is easy to set up and use. Python's sqlite3 module provides a way to interact with SQLite databases.

- **Creating and Connecting to a Database:**

python
```
import sqlite3

# Connect to the database (or create it if it doesn't exist)
conn = sqlite3.connect('example.db')
```

```
cursor = conn.cursor()
```

- **Creating a Table:**

python
```
cursor.execute('''
    CREATE TABLE IF NOT EXISTS users (
        id INTEGER PRIMARY KEY,
        name TEXT,
        age INTEGER,
        email TEXT
    )
''')
conn.commit()
```

19.4 Performing CRUD Operations

CRUD (Create, Read, Update, Delete) operations are the basic functions of persistent storage.

- **Inserting Data (Create):**

python
```
cursor.execute('''
    INSERT INTO users (name, age, email) VALUES (?, ?, ?)
''', ('Alice', 30, 'alice@example.com'))
conn.commit()
```

- **Retrieving Data (Read):**

python
```
cursor.execute('SELECT * FROM users')
rows = cursor.fetchall()
for row in rows:
    print(row)
```

- **Updating Data (Update):**

python
```
cursor.execute('''
    UPDATE users SET age = ? WHERE name = ?
''', (31, 'Alice'))
conn.commit()
```

- **Deleting Data (Delete):**

python
```
cursor.execute('''
    DELETE FROM users WHERE name = ?
''', ('Alice',))
```

```
conn.commit()
```

19.5 Using ORM with SQLAlchemy

Object-Relational Mapping (ORM) is a technique that allows you to interact with a database using Python objects, rather than writing raw SQL queries. SQLAlchemy is a popular ORM library for Python.

- **Installing SQLAlchemy:**

bash
```
pip install sqlalchemy
```

- **Setting Up SQLAlchemy:**

python
```
from sqlalchemy import create_engine, Column, Integer, String
from sqlalchemy.ext.declarative import declarative_base
from sqlalchemy.orm import sessionmaker

# Create an engine and a base class
engine = create_engine('sqlite:///example.db')
Base = declarative_base()

# Define a User model
class User(Base):
    __tablename__ = 'users'
    id = Column(Integer, primary_key=True)
    name = Column(String)
    age = Column(Integer)
    email = Column(String)

# Create the table
Base.metadata.create_all(engine)

# Create a session
Session = sessionmaker(bind=engine)
session = Session()
```

- **Performing CRUD Operations with SQLAlchemy:**
  - **Inserting Data (Create):**

python
```
new_user = User(name='Bob', age=25, email='bob@example.com')
session.add(new_user)
session.commit()
```

  - **Retrieving Data (Read):**

python
```
users = session.query(User).all()
for user in users:
    print(user.name, user.age, user.email)
```

- **Updating Data (Update):**

python
```
user = session.query(User).filter_by(name='Bob').first()
user.age = 26
session.commit()
```

- **Deleting Data (Delete):**

python
```
user = session.query(User).filter_by(name='Bob').first()
session.delete(user)
session.commit()
```

Understanding databases and SQL is essential for managing and manipulating data efficiently. By leveraging SQLite and SQLAlchemy, you can perform CRUD operations and interact with databases seamlessly within your Python applications.

CHAPTER 20: GUI DEVELOPMENT WITH TKINTER

20.1 Introduction to Tkinter

Tkinter is the standard GUI (Graphical User Interface) library for Python, providing a fast and easy way to create GUI applications. It comes bundled with Python, so you don't need to install anything extra.

20.2 Creating Windows and Widgets

Tkinter provides various widgets (controls) such as buttons, labels, text boxes, and more to build interactive interfaces.

- **Creating a Basic Window:**

python
```
import tkinter as tk

# Create the main window
root = tk.Tk()
root.title("My First GUI")
root.geometry("400x300")

# Run the main event loop
root.mainloop()
```

- **Adding a Label:**

python
```
import tkinter as tk

root = tk.Tk()
root.title("Label Example")
root.geometry("300x200")
```

```
# Create and place a label
label = tk.Label(root, text="Hello, Tkinter!")
label.pack()

root.mainloop()
```

- **Adding a Button:**

python
```
import tkinter as tk

def on_click():
    print("Button clicked!")

root = tk.Tk()
root.title("Button Example")
root.geometry("300x200")

# Create and place a button
button = tk.Button(root, text="Click Me", command=on_click)
button.pack()

root.mainloop()
```

20.3 Event Handling

Event handling in Tkinter allows your application to respond to user interactions such as button clicks, key presses, and mouse movements.

- **Handling Button Clicks:**

python
```
import tkinter as tk

def on_click():
    label.config(text="Button clicked!")

root = tk.Tk()
root.title("Event Handling Example")
root.geometry("300x200")

label = tk.Label(root, text="Click the button")
label.pack()

button = tk.Button(root, text="Click Me", command=on_click)
button.pack()

root.mainloop()
```

- **Handling Keyboard Events:**

python
```
import tkinter as tk

def on_key_press(event):
    label.config(text=f"Key pressed: {event.char}")

root = tk.Tk()
root.title("Keyboard Event Example")
root.geometry("300x200")

label = tk.Label(root, text="Press a key")
label.pack()

root.bind("<KeyPress>", on_key_press)

root.mainloop()
```

20.4 Layout Management

Tkinter provides three layout managers to control the placement of widgets: pack, grid, and place.

- **Using Pack:**

python
```
import tkinter as tk

root = tk.Tk()
root.title("Pack Layout")
root.geometry("300x200")

label1 = tk.Label(root, text="Label 1")
label1.pack(side=tk.TOP)

label2 = tk.Label(root, text="Label 2")
label2.pack(side=tk.BOTTOM)

root.mainloop()
```

- **Using Grid:**

python
```
import tkinter as tk

root = tk.Tk()
root.title("Grid Layout")
root.geometry("300x200")

label1 = tk.Label(root, text="Label 1")
```

```python
label1.grid(row=0, column=0)

label2 = tk.Label(root, text="Label 2")
label2.grid(row=1, column=1)

root.mainloop()
```

- **Using Place:**

```python
import tkinter as tk

root = tk.Tk()
root.title("Place Layout")
root.geometry("300x200")

label = tk.Label(root, text="This is placed using coordinates.")
label.place(x=50, y=50)

root.mainloop()
```

20.5 Building a Simple GUI Application

Let's build a simple calculator using Tkinter to demonstrate how to combine various widgets and event handling.

- **Simple Calculator:**

```python
import tkinter as tk

def add_numbers():
    num1 = float(entry1.get())
    num2 = float(entry2.get())
    result = num1 + num2
    result_label.config(text=f"Result: {result}")

root = tk.Tk()
root.title("Simple Calculator")
root.geometry("300x200")

entry1 = tk.Entry(root)
entry1.pack()

entry2 = tk.Entry(root)
entry2.pack()

add_button = tk.Button(root, text="Add", command=add_numbers)
add_button.pack()

result_label = tk.Label(root, text="Result: ")
```

```
result_label.pack()

root.mainloop()
```

GUI development with Tkinter allows you to create user-friendly interfaces for your Python applications. By mastering the creation and placement of widgets, event handling, and layout management, you can build interactive and responsive GUI applications.

CHAPTER 21: NETWORK PROGRAMMING

21.1 Introduction to Network Programming

Network programming involves writing code that enables computers to communicate over a network. This can be as simple as sending and receiving data between two computers or as complex as building a distributed system. Python's standard library provides extensive support for network programming.

21.2 Basics of Network Programming

Networks operate based on protocols, which are sets of rules defining how data is exchanged. The most commonly used protocol for network communication is TCP/IP.

- **Client-Server Model:**
  - **Client:** Initiates the communication.
  - **Server:** Responds to the client's requests.

21.3 Working with Sockets

Sockets are the endpoints of a bidirectional communication link between two programs running on a network. Python's socket module provides access to the BSD socket interface.

- **Creating a Socket:**

python
```
import socket

# Create a socket object
s = socket.socket(socket.AF_INET, socket.SOCK_STREAM)
```

- ### **Connecting to a Server:**

python

```python
import socket

# Create a socket object
s = socket.socket(socket.AF_INET, socket.SOCK_STREAM)

# Define the server address and port
server_address = ('localhost', 8080)

# Connect to the server
s.connect(server_address)

# Send data
message = 'Hello, Server!'
s.sendall(message.encode('utf-8'))

# Receive response
data = s.recv(1024)
print('Received from server:', data.decode('utf-8'))

# Close the connection
s.close()
```

- ### **Creating a Server:**

python

```python
import socket

# Create a socket object
s = socket.socket(socket.AF_INET, socket.SOCK_STREAM)

# Bind the socket to the address and port
server_address = ('localhost', 8080)
s.bind(server_address)

# Listen for incoming connections
s.listen(1)
print('Server listening on', server_address)

# Accept a connection
conn, addr = s.accept()
print('Connected by', addr)

# Receive data
data = conn.recv(1024)
print('Received:', data.decode('utf-8'))
```

```python
# Send response
conn.sendall('Hello, Client!'.encode('utf-8'))

# Close the connection
conn.close()
```

21.4 Creating a Simple Client-Server Application

A simple client-server application demonstrates the basic principles of network programming.

- **Client Code:**

python
```python
import socket

def client_program():
    host = 'localhost'
    port = 5000

    client_socket = socket.socket(socket.AF_INET, socket.SOCK_STREAM)
    client_socket.connect((host, port))

    message = input(" -> ")  # Take input

    while message.lower().strip() != 'bye':
        client_socket.send(message.encode())
        data = client_socket.recv(1024).decode()

        print('Received from server: ' + data)

        message = input(" -> ")  # Again take input

    client_socket.close()

if __name__ == '__main__':
    client_program()
```

- **Server Code:**

python
```python
import socket

def server_program():
    host = 'localhost'
    port = 5000

    server_socket = socket.socket(socket.AF_INET, socket.SOCK_STREAM)
    server_socket.bind((host, port))

    server_socket.listen(2)
```

```
    conn, address = server_socket.accept()
    print("Connection from: " + str(address))

    while True:
        data = conn.recv(1024).decode()
        if not data:
            break
        print("Received from client: " + str(data))
        data = input(' -> ')
        conn.send(data.encode())

    conn.close()

if __name__ == '__main__':
    server_program()
```

21.5 Handling HTTP Requests

Python provides libraries like requests and http.server to handle HTTP requests and build simple web servers.

- **Using the Requests Library:**

python
```
import requests

response = requests.get('https://jsonplaceholder.typicode.com/posts')
print(response.json())
```

- **Creating a Simple HTTP Server:**

python
```
from http.server import SimpleHTTPRequestHandler, HTTPServer

class MyHandler(SimpleHTTPRequestHandler):
    def do_GET(self):
        self.send_response(200)
        self.send_header('Content-type', 'text/html')
        self.end_headers()
        self.wfile.write(b'Hello, World!')

server_address = ('', 8000)
httpd = HTTPServer(server_address, MyHandler)
print('Server running on port 8000...')
httpd.serve_forever()
```

Network programming in Python allows you to build applications that communicate over the internet or local networks. By understanding sockets, the client-server model, and handling

HTTP requests, you can create robust networked applications.

CHAPTER 22: MULTITHREADING AND MULTIPROCESSING

22.1 Introduction to Concurrent Programming

Concurrent programming involves executing multiple tasks simultaneously to make better use of system resources and improve performance. Python provides two main approaches to concurrency: multithreading and multiprocessing.

- **Multithreading:** Involves multiple threads within a single process.
- **Multiprocessing:** Involves multiple processes, each with its own memory space.

22.2 Understanding Threads and Processes

- **Threads:** A thread is the smallest unit of execution within a process. Threads within the same process share the same memory space.
- **Processes:** A process is an independent program that runs in its own memory space. Multiple processes can run concurrently on a multicore processor.

22.3 Using the threading Module

The threading module in Python provides a way to create and manage threads. It allows you to execute multiple threads (tasks, function calls) at the same time.

- **Creating and Starting a Thread:**

```python
import threading

def print_numbers():
    for i in range(1, 6):
        print(i)

thread = threading.Thread(target=print_numbers)
thread.start()
thread.join() # Wait for the thread to finish
```

- **Using a Thread Class:**

```python
import threading

class PrintNumbers(threading.Thread):
    def run(self):
        for i in range(1, 6):
            print(i)

thread = PrintNumbers()
thread.start()
thread.join()
```

22.4 Synchronization with Locks

When multiple threads access shared resources, synchronization is necessary to prevent data corruption. The threading module provides locks for this purpose.

- **Using Locks:**

```python
import threading

lock = threading.Lock()
counter = 0

def increment():
    global counter
    with lock:
        counter += 1

threads = [threading.Thread(target=increment) for _ in range(100)]
for thread in threads:
    thread.start()
```

```
for thread in threads:
    thread.join()
```

```
print("Final counter value:", counter)
```

22.5 Using the multiprocessing Module

The multiprocessing module in Python allows you to create and manage processes, providing an alternative to threading for CPU-bound tasks.

- **Creating and Starting a Process:**

python
```
import multiprocessing

def print_numbers():
    for i in range(1, 6):
        print(i)

process = multiprocessing.Process(target=print_numbers)
process.start()
process.join()
```

- **Using a Process Class:**

python
```
import multiprocessing

class PrintNumbers(multiprocessing.Process):
    def run(self):
        for i in range(1, 6):
            print(i)

process = PrintNumbers()
process.start()
process.join()
```

22.6 Inter-process Communication

The multiprocessing module provides mechanisms for communication between processes, such as queues and pipes.

- **Using Queues:**

python
```
import multiprocessing

def worker(queue):
    queue.put("Data from worker")
```

```
queue = multiprocessing.Queue()
process = multiprocessing.Process(target=worker, args=(queue,))
process.start()
print(queue.get()) # Output: Data from worker
process.join()
```

- **Using Pipes:**

python
```
import multiprocessing

def worker(pipe):
    pipe.send("Data from worker")
    pipe.close()

parent_conn, child_conn = multiprocessing.Pipe()
process = multiprocessing.Process(target=worker, args=(child_conn,))
process.start()
print(parent_conn.recv()) # Output: Data from worker
process.join()
```

22.7 Synchronization with Manager

The multiprocessing module provides a Manager class to manage shared resources between processes.

- **Using a Manager:**

python
```
import multiprocessing

def worker(shared_list, shared_dict):
    shared_list.append(1)
    shared_dict["key"] = "value"

manager = multiprocessing.Manager()
shared_list = manager.list()
shared_dict = manager.dict()

processes = [multiprocessing.Process(target=worker, args=(shared_list,
shared_dict)) for _ in range(10)]
for process in processes:
    process.start()
for process in processes:
    process.join()

print(shared_list) # Output: [1, 1, 1, 1, 1, 1, 1, 1, 1, 1]
print(shared_dict) # Output: {'key': 'value'}
```

22.8 Choosing Between Multithreading and Multiprocessing

- **Multithreading:** Suitable for I/O-bound tasks such as file I/O, network operations, and user interaction.

- **Multiprocessing:** Suitable for CPU-bound tasks such as mathematical computations, image processing, and data analysis.

Multithreading and multiprocessing are powerful techniques for improving the performance of Python applications by enabling concurrent execution of tasks. Understanding when to use each approach and how to manage synchronization and communication between threads and processes is essential for developing efficient and robust applications.

CHAPTER 23:
UNIT TESTING

23.1 Importance of Testing

Unit testing is the process of testing individual units or components of a software to ensure they work as expected. It is crucial for maintaining code quality, detecting bugs early, and ensuring that changes do not break existing functionality.

23.2 Writing Unit Tests with unittest

Python's unittest module, inspired by Java's JUnit, is a standard framework for writing and running tests.

- **Creating a Test Case:**

python
```python
import unittest

def add(a, b):
    return a + b

class TestMathFunctions(unittest.TestCase):
    def test_add(self):
        self.assertEqual(add(3, 4), 7)
        self.assertEqual(add(-1, 1), 0)

if __name__ == '__main__':
    unittest.main()
```

- **Running Tests:** Save the test script as test_math_functions.py and run it from the command line:

bash
```bash
python test_math_functions.py
```

23.3 Using pytest for Testing

pytest is a popular third-party testing framework that offers a simpler syntax and many powerful features.

- **Installing pytest:**

bash
```
pip install pytest
```

- **Writing a Test with pytest:**

python
```
def add(a, b):
    return a + b

def test_add():
    assert add(3, 4) == 7
    assert add(-1, 1) == 0
```

- **Running Tests with pytest:** Save the test script as test_math_functions.py and run it using pytest:

bash
```
pytest test_math_functions.py
```

23.4 Test-Driven Development (TDD)

Test-Driven Development (TDD) is a software development process in which tests are written before writing the actual code. The cycle typically involves writing a failing test, writing the minimum code to pass the test, and then refactoring the code.

- **TDD Cycle:**
    1. Write a test for a new feature.
    2. Run the test (it should fail since the feature isn't implemented yet).
    3. Implement the feature.
    4. Run the test again (it should pass now).
    5. Refactor the code if necessary.
    6. Repeat.

- **Example of TDD:**

python
```
import unittest

def add(a, b):
    return a + b  # Initial implementation
```

```
class TestMathFunctions(unittest.TestCase):
    def test_add(self):
        self.assertEqual(add(3, 4), 7)
        self.assertEqual(add(-1, 1), 0)

if __name__ == '__main__':
    unittest.main()
```

Write the test first, run it to see it fail, implement the feature, and then run the test again to see it pass.

23.5 Mocking

Mocking is a technique used to replace real objects with mock objects during testing. It is useful for isolating the code under test and for simulating different scenarios.

- **Using unittest.mock:**

python
```
from unittest.mock import Mock

# Mocking a function
mock_function = Mock(return_value=10)
print(mock_function()) # Output: 10

# Mocking a method in a class
class MyClass:
    def method(self):
        pass

my_instance = MyClass()
my_instance.method = Mock(return_value="Mocked")
print(my_instance.method()) # Output: Mocked
```

23.6 Fixtures and Setup/Teardown Methods

Fixtures are used to set up the environment for tests. They help to prepare the necessary preconditions and clean up after the tests.

- **Using unittest Setup/Teardown:**

python
```
import unittest

class TestExample(unittest.TestCase):
    def setUp(self):
        # Code to set up test environment
        pass
```

```python
    def tearDown(self):
        # Code to clean up after tests
        pass

    def test_example(self):
        # Test code
        pass

if __name__ == '__main__':
    unittest.main()
```

- **Using pytest Fixtures:**

python
```python
import pytest

@pytest.fixture
def setup_data():
    # Setup code
    data = "sample data"
    yield data
    # Teardown code

def test_example(setup_data):
    assert setup_data == "sample data"
```

Unit testing is a critical practice for ensuring the reliability and maintainability of your code. By leveraging tools like unittest and pytest, and adopting techniques like TDD and mocking, you can write robust and comprehensive tests that help you catch bugs early and maintain high-quality code.

CHAPTER 24: WORKING WITH VIRTUAL ENVIRONMENTS

24.1 Introduction to Virtual Environments

A virtual environment is an isolated Python environment that allows you to manage dependencies for different projects separately. This is crucial for avoiding conflicts between packages required for different projects and ensuring consistent and reproducible environments.

24.2 Creating Virtual Environments

Python's venv module provides a simple way to create virtual environments.

- **Creating a Virtual Environment:**

bash
```
python -m venv myenv
```

This command creates a new directory named myenv containing a copy of the Python interpreter and standard library.

24.3 Activating and Deactivating Virtual Environments

Once created, the virtual environment needs to be activated before you can use it.

- **Activating on Windows:**

bash
myenv\Scripts\activate

- **Activating on macOS/Linux:**

bash
source myenv/bin/activate

- **Deactivating a Virtual Environment:**

bash
deactivate

24.4 Managing Packages

Within an active virtual environment, you can use pip to install, upgrade, and remove packages.

- **Installing Packages:**

bash
pip install requests

- **Upgrading Packages:**

bash
pip install --upgrade requests

- **Uninstalling Packages:**

bash
pip uninstall requests

24.5 Using a Requirements File

A requirements file lists all the dependencies for a project, allowing you to easily recreate the environment on another system.

- **Creating a Requirements File:**

bash
pip freeze > requirements.txt

- **Installing from a Requirements File:**

bash
pip install -r requirements.txt

24.6 Best Practices for Dependencies Management

Managing dependencies efficiently ensures the smooth functioning of your projects and avoids conflicts.

- **Isolate Each Project:** Create a separate virtual environment for each project to prevent dependency conflicts.

- **Use Requirements Files:** Keep an up-to-date requirements file for each project to ensure reproducibility.

- **Regularly Update Dependencies:** Periodically update dependencies to incorporate bug fixes and new features, but ensure compatibility with your project.

- **Use Version Control:** Specify exact versions of dependencies in the requirements file to avoid unexpected changes.

24.7 Alternatives to venv

While venv is sufficient for most needs, other tools offer additional features for managing virtual environments.

- **virtualenv:** An alternative to venv with additional features.

bash
```
pip install virtualenv
virtualenv myenv
source myenv/bin/activate  # Activate the environment
```

- **pipenv:** Combines pip and virtualenv to provide a streamlined workflow for managing dependencies.

bash
```
pip install pipenv
pipenv install requests  # Creates a virtual environment and installs the package
pipenv shell  # Activates the environment
```

Virtual environments are essential for managing dependencies and ensuring consistency across different projects. By following best practices and using tools like venv, virtualenv, and pipenv, you can effectively manage and isolate your project's environment.

CHAPTER 25: DEPLOYMENT AND DISTRIBUTION

25.1 Introduction to Deployment

Deployment involves preparing and releasing software for use in a production environment. Proper deployment ensures that your application runs smoothly and securely on the target infrastructure. It includes tasks like packaging, configuring environments, and automating deployment processes.

25.2 Preparing Code for Deployment

Before deploying, ensure your code is clean, well-documented, and tested.

- **Code Review:** Conduct thorough code reviews to catch bugs and improve code quality.
- **Documentation:** Document your code, including usage instructions and dependencies.
- **Testing:** Run all unit tests and integration tests to ensure everything works as expected.

25.3 Packaging Python Applications

Packaging your application involves bundling your code and dependencies into a format that can be easily installed and executed.

- **Creating a setup.py File:**

python
```
from setuptools import setup, find_packages
```

```
setup(
    name="myapp",
    version="1.0",
    packages=find_packages(),
    install_requires=[
        "requests",
        "numpy",
    ],
    entry_points={
        "console_scripts": [
            "myapp = myapp.main:main",
        ],
    },
)
```

- **Building the Package:**

bash
```
python setup.py sdist bdist_wheel
```

- **Installing the Package:**

bash
```
pip install .
```

25.4 Publishing Packages to PyPI

The Python Package Index (PyPI) is a repository for Python packages. Publishing your package to PyPI makes it accessible to others.

- **Registering on PyPI:** Create an account on PyPI.
- **Uploading the Package:**

bash
```
pip install twine
twine upload dist/*
```

25.5 Continuous Integration and Deployment (CI/CD)

CI/CD automates the process of testing, building, and deploying code, ensuring consistent and reliable releases.

- **Setting Up CI/CD with GitHub Actions:** Create a .github/workflows/ci.yml file in your repository.

yaml
```
name: CI
```

```
on: [push, pull_request]

jobs:
  build:
    runs-on: ubuntu-latest

    steps:
    - uses: actions/checkout@v2
    - name: Set up Python
      uses: actions/setup-python@v2
      with:
        python-version: '3.x'
    - name: Install dependencies
      run: |
        python -m pip install --upgrade pip
        pip install -r requirements.txt
    - name: Run tests
      run: |
        pytest
```

- **Setting Up Deployment with GitHub Actions:** Extend the CI workflow to include deployment steps.

yaml
```
name: CI/CD

on: [push]

jobs:
  build:
    runs-on: ubuntu-latest

    steps:
    - uses: actions/checkout@v2
    - name: Set up Python
      uses: actions/setup-python@v2
      with:
        python-version: '3.x'
    - name: Install dependencies
      run: |
        python -m pip install --upgrade pip
        pip install -r requirements.txt
    - name: Run tests
      run: |
        pytest

  deploy:
```

```
runs-on: ubuntu-latest
needs: build

steps:
- uses: actions/checkout@v2
- name: Deploy to server
  run: |
    ssh user@server "cd /path/to/app && git pull && ./deploy.sh"
```

25.6 Best Practices for Deployment

- **Environment Configuration:** Use environment variables to manage configuration settings.

- **Monitoring and Logging:** Implement monitoring and logging to track the application's performance and troubleshoot issues.

- **Automated Backups:** Set up automated backups for critical data and configurations.

- **Scalability:** Design your deployment process to handle increased load and scale resources as needed.

Deploying and distributing Python applications involves preparing your code, packaging it, and using tools like CI/CD to automate the process. By following best practices and leveraging tools like PyPI and GitHub Actions, you can ensure smooth and reliable deployments.

CHAPTER 26: ADVANCED PYTHON TECHNIQUES

26.1 Decorators

Decorators are a powerful and expressive tool in Python that allow you to modify the behavior of functions or methods. They are commonly used for logging, enforcing access control, instrumentation, and caching.

- **Creating a Decorator:**

python
```python
def my_decorator(func):
    def wrapper():
        print("Something is happening before the function is called.")
        func()
        print("Something is happening after the function is called.")
    return wrapper

@my_decorator
def say_hello():
    print("Hello!")

say_hello()
```

- **Decorating Functions with Arguments:**

python
```python
def my_decorator(func):
    def wrapper(*args, **kwargs):
        print("Something is happening before the function is called.")
        result = func(*args, **kwargs)
        print("Something is happening after the function is called.")
        return result
```

```
    return wrapper

@my_decorator
def greet(name):
    print(f"Hello, {name}!")

greet("Alice")
```

26.2 Context Managers

Context managers allow you to allocate and release resources precisely when you want to. The most common use of context managers is the with statement.

- **Using** with **Statement:**

python
```
with open('example.txt', 'w') as file:
    file.write('Hello, World!')
```

- **Creating a Context Manager:**

python
```
class MyContextManager:
    def __enter__(self):
        print("Entering the context")
        return self

    def __exit__(self, exc_type, exc_value, traceback):
        print("Exiting the context")

with MyContextManager():
    print("Inside the context")
```

- **Context Manager using** contextlib:

python
```
from contextlib import contextmanager

@contextmanager
def my_context():
    print("Entering the context")
    yield
    print("Exiting the context")

with my_context():
    print("Inside the context")
```

26.3 Generators

Generators are a simple way of creating iterators using a function that yields values one at a time.

- **Creating a Generator:**

python
```
def count_up_to(max):
    count = 1
    while count <= max:
        yield count
        count += 1

counter = count_up_to(5)
for number in counter:
    print(number)
```

- **Generator Expressions:**

python
```
squares = (x * x for x in range(10))
for square in squares:
    print(square)
```

26.4 Metaclasses

Metaclasses are classes of classes that define how classes behave. They can be used to customize class creation.

- **Basic Metaclass Example:**

python
```
class Meta(type):
    def __new__(cls, name, bases, dct):
        print(f"Creating class {name}")
        return super().__new__(cls, name, bases, dct)

class MyClass(metaclass=Meta):
    pass
```

- **Customizing Class Creation:**

python
```
class Meta(type):
    def __new__(cls, name, bases, dct):
        dct['custom_attribute'] = 'Hello, World!'
        return super().__new__(cls, name, bases, dct)

class MyClass(metaclass=Meta):
    pass

instance = MyClass()
```

```
print(instance.custom_attribute)
```

26.5 Type Hints and Annotations

Type hints and annotations provide a way to specify the expected types of variables, function parameters, and return values.

- **Using Type Hints:**

python
```
def add(a: int, b: int) -> int:
    return a + b

def greet(name: str) -> str:
    return f"Hello, {name}!"
```

- **Type Checking with** mypy**:**

bash
```
pip install mypy
mypy myscript.py
```

Advanced Python techniques like decorators, context managers, generators, metaclasses, and type hints enable you to write more powerful, flexible, and maintainable code. By mastering these concepts, you can take full advantage of Python's capabilities and improve your programming skills.

CHAPTER 27: WORKING WITH TIME AND DATES

27.1 Introduction to Time and Dates in Python

Handling time and dates is crucial for many applications, such as logging events, scheduling tasks, and analyzing time-series data. Python provides several modules to work with dates and times, including datetime, time, and calendar.

27.2 The datetime Module

The datetime module supplies classes for manipulating dates and times in a simple and complex way. It allows arithmetic operations on dates and times and provides various formatting options.

- **Creating Date and Time Objects:**

python
```
from datetime import datetime, date, time

# Current date and time
now = datetime.now()
print(now)

# Create a specific date
d = date(2023, 12, 21)
print(d)

# Create a specific time
t = time(14, 30)
print(t)
```

- **Formatting Dates and Times:**

python
```
# Format the current date and time
formatted_now = now.strftime("%Y-%m-%d %H:%M:%S")
print(formatted_now)

# Parse a string into a datetime object
date_str = "2023-12-21 14:30:00"
parsed_date = datetime.strptime(date_str, "%Y-%m-%d %H:%M:%S")
print(parsed_date)
```

- **Date and Time Arithmetic:**

python
```
from datetime import timedelta

# Adding 10 days to the current date
future_date = now + timedelta(days=10)
print(future_date)

# Subtracting 2 hours from the current time
past_time = now - timedelta(hours=2)
print(past_time)
```

27.3 The time Module

The time module provides time-related functions. It is less versatile than the datetime module but still useful for certain tasks, such as measuring elapsed time.

- **Getting the Current Time:**

python
```
import time

# Current time in seconds since the epoch
current_time = time.time()
print(current_time)

# Convert seconds to a struct_time
local_time = time.localtime(current_time)
print(local_time)

# Format the struct_time
formatted_time = time.strftime("%Y-%m-%d %H:%M:%S", local_time)
print(formatted_time)
```

- **Sleeping:**

python
```
# Sleep for 2 seconds
```

```
time.sleep(2)
print("2 seconds have passed")
```

27.4 The calendar Module

The calendar module provides functions related to the calendar, such as checking leap years and generating calendar data.

- **Checking for Leap Year:**

python
```
import calendar

year = 2024
is_leap = calendar.isleap(year)
print(f"Is {year} a leap year? {is_leap}")
```

- **Printing a Month's Calendar:**

python
```
year = 2023
month = 12
print(calendar.month(year, month))
```

- **Printing a Year's Calendar:**

python
```
year = 2023
print(calendar.calendar(year))
```

27.5 Time Zones and Daylight Saving Time

Handling time zones and daylight saving time (DST) can be complex. The pytz library helps manage time zones more effectively.

- **Installing pytz:**

bash
```
pip install pytz
```

- **Working with Time Zones:**

python
```
from datetime import datetime
import pytz

# Create a timezone object
timezone = pytz.timezone("America/New_York")

# Localize a datetime object to the specified timezone
local_time = timezone.localize(datetime.now())
```

```
print(local_time)

# Convert to another timezone
utc_time = local_time.astimezone(pytz.utc)
print(utc_time)
```

Handling time and dates in Python is essential for many applications. By leveraging the datetime, time, and calendar modules, and using libraries like pytz for time zone management, you can efficiently work with time and dates in your programs.

ACKNOWLEDGEMENT

Writing this book, **"Mastering Python: From Basics to Advanced Techniques"**, has been an incredible journey, and it would not have been possible without the support, guidance, and encouragement of many people.

First and foremost, I would like to express my deepest gratitude to my family for their unwavering support and understanding throughout the writing process. Your patience and encouragement have been invaluable to me.

I am profoundly grateful to my mentors and colleagues, whose insights and feedback have greatly enriched the content of this book. Your expertise and constructive criticism have been instrumental in shaping this work into a comprehensive guide for Python enthusiasts.

A special thanks to the Python community, whose contributions and collaborative spirit have made Python the versatile and robust language it is today. The wealth of resources, discussions, and shared knowledge within the community has been a constant source of inspiration.

I would also like to extend my heartfelt appreciation to the reviewers and editors who meticulously went through the manuscript, offering valuable suggestions and corrections. Your attention to detail and commitment to excellence have significantly enhanced the quality of this book.

Finally, I am immensely grateful to the readers. Your curiosity and passion for learning are what drive the creation of educational resources like this one. I hope this book serves as a valuable tool in your journey to mastering Python.

Thank you all for your support, encouragement, and contributions.

www.ingramcontent.com/pod-product-compliance
Lightning Source LLC
LaVergne TN
LVHW022353060326
832902LV00022B/4424